ALFRED'S
DRUM SHOP *Series*

MW00784094

THE DRUMMER'S TOOLKIT

the most complete reference guide available

- Tuning and arranging your drumset for personal efficiency
- Selecting cymbals, drumheads, mallets and drumsticks
- Care and maintenance
- Practice tips and glossary of terms

Cover photo courtesy of Yamaha Corporation of America.
Photos on p. 18 (bottom) by Karen Miller.
Photos on p. 20 (top), 23, 24, 25, and 26 by Jeff Leland.
Photos of Yamaha drums and hardware courtesy of Yamaha Corporation of America.
Photos of Sabian cymbals and hardware courtesy of Sabian Inc.
Drumhead photos on p. 6 courtesy of Remo Inc.
Drumhead photos on p. 7 courtesy of Evans Drumheads.

Dave Black

Alfred

CONTENTS

PREFACE

The Drummer's Toolkit is a well-organized reference guide for drum students, professionals and educators alike. Written in an easy-to-use, step-by-step format that includes lots of photographs and diagrams, this one-stop sourcebook covers everything you need to know to effectively and consistently tune your drums and set up your drumset.

Part one covers topics including drumhead selection, changing a drumhead, tuning your drums, and important concepts such as muffling and obtaining the correct drum sound. Part two continues with the parts of the drumset and each drum, arranging the drumset for personal efficiency, additional cymbal types, drumstick and mallet selection, general practice tips, and care and maintenance. Readers are encouraged to experiment on their own, as such creativity is essential to finding out what works best.

The following material is presented in an interesting and satisfying manner, ensuring you'll find this resource guide helpful in your pursuit of musical excellence.

ABOUT THE AUTHOR

Percussionist/composer Dave Black received his Bachelor of Music in percussion performance from California State University, Northridge.   While at Northridge, he studied with notable teachers and performers such as Louie Bellson, Joel Leach, Ed Shaughnessy, Steve Schaeffer, Jerry Steinholtz and the late Nick Ceroli. He has traveled around the world with a variety of entertainers and shows, performing and recording with such artists as Alan King, Robert Merrill, June Allyson, Anita O'Day, Pete Jolly, Frankie Capp, Gordon Brisker, Kim Richmond, Victor Lewis, Jerry Hey and Steve Huffsteter.

A prolific composer and arranger, more than 50 of his compositions and arrangements have been published by Alfred Publishing, Barnhouse, CPP/Belwin, TRN, Highland/Etling and Warner Brothers, and many of them have been recorded. Mr. Black has written with, and for the bands of Louie Bellson, Sammy Nestico, Bill Watrous, Bobby Shew, Ed Shaughnessy, Gordon Brisker and the C.S.U., Northridge Jazz Ensemble. He has been the recipient of many awards and commissions, including 13 consecutive ASCAP Popular Composer Awards (for his contributions to the symphonic and concert repertoires) and two Grammy participation/nomination certificates—one for his performance contribution on Anita O'Day's Grammy-nominated album *In a Mellow Tone,* and the other for his contribution as album-track composer on Louie Bellson's Grammy-nominated album *Airmail Special.*   In addition, many of his compositions have been used as source/background music on numerous TV shows including *All My Children, Coach, The Drew Carey Show, General Hospital, Ellen, Grace Under Fire, Nightline, Roseanne* and *Good Morning America.*

Mr. Black is the co-author of several best-selling books published by Alfred Publishing Company: *Alfred's Drum Method, Books 1 & 2* (the world's current best seller); *Alfred's Beginning Drumset Method; Contemporary Brush Techniques; Alfred's Beginning Snare Drum Duets; Cymbals: A Crash Course; A Jazz Diary* (chosen for the 1998–2000 National Federation of Music Club's Junior Festival Bulletin); *Drumset Independence & Syncopation;* and *The Essential Dictionary of Orchestration.* His books and music are used and performed by tens of thousands of young people all over the world. He has also written countless articles, book reviews and concert reviews for prominent magazines such as *Down Beat, The Instrumentalist, Modern Drummer, Modern Percussionist, Drums and Drumming, Drum Tracks, Grammy Pulse, Jazz Educators Journal* and *Music Connection*—in addition to being a featured subject in many of them.

As an active member of the Percussive Arts Society (PAS), Mr. Black served on the National Board of Directors for six years, was a member of the Sustaining Members Advisory Council, and was selected to host/chair the 1991 Percussive Arts Society International Convention in Anaheim, California. He presently serves as the Director of Instrumental Music for Alfred Publishing Company.

Acknowledgements

Special thanks to Dave Tull, Rod Harbour, Dave White, Rich Lackowski, Kate Westin, Link Harnsberger, Kalani; Lloyd McCausland at Remo, Inc.; Mike Robinson at Evans Drumheads; Sabian Ltd.; and Joe Testa at Yamaha Corp. of America.

PART 1 HOW TO TUNE YOUR DRUMS

The most important aspect of drumset tuning is the balance that needs to exist between the components of the set. The determined pitch will depend largely on the style of music being played and the player's own personal taste. For example, rock styles most often employ a low, punchy tuning, whereas jazz styles tend to use mid- to high-pitched tunings. Tuning and muffling should be checked behind the drumset as well as from the vantage point of the audience. A fair amount of experimentation will be required to find what works best for you.

There are two methods for tuning drums: the *cross-tension system,* and the *clockwise system* of tensioning. The clockwise system of tensioning is the less useful of the two, as the head tends to wrinkle in undesirable places and does not sit properly on the bearing edge. This method of tuning is therefore inconsistent and undependable. By contrast, the cross-tension system maintains even tensioning around the drum throughout the entire tuning process.

THE DRUM AND ITS PARTS

Many parts are common to all drums of a drumset. The snare drum is used here as a model for pointing out the various features. Parts specific to individual drums are addressed in the appropriate sections.

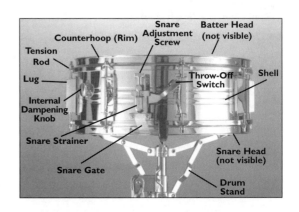

1. The top head of the snare drum is referred to as the *batter head,* and is available with either a smooth finish or rough, sand-like coating. The bottom head is called the *snare head*. As a general rule, the bottom head should be thinner and slightly tighter than the batter head. In most cases, the batter head will determine the timbre of the drum, but this, of course, will depend on the thickness, resonance and condition of the head.

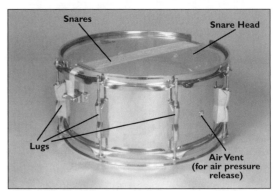

2. The *flesh hoop* (originally a wooden piece around which damp calfskin was tucked) is a ring, usually metal, to which the head is attached by means of glue or pressure.

3. Drumheads are held in place by *counterhoops,* also referred to as *rims*. They are made of either metal or wood and sit on top of the flesh hoop, holding the head onto the rim with the help of *tension rods.*

4. The *shell* is the frame that supports all the other components of the drum. It may be constructed of wood, sometimes with a lacquer or pearl finish, or made of metal or fiberglass.

5. The *bearing edge* is the point on the snare drum where the head meets the rim. Usually cut at a 45-degree angle, this edge must evenly touch the drumhead to insure its proper seating on the shell.

6. *Lugs* are attached to the side of the drum shell and serve as receptacles for the tension rods.

7. *Tension rods* hold the counterhoop in place and are used to adjust the tension of the drumhead. The number of rods and lugs attached to the snare drum depends upon the size of the drum, but the usual number is 8 to10 for most drums.

8. The *air vent* is a hole in the side of the drum shell that allows air to escape when the batter head is struck.

9. The *snare strainer,* also called the *snare release,* allows the snares to be engaged or disengaged from the snare head by means of a throw-off switch.

10. The *tension adjustment knob* is located on top of the throw-off switch. Turning it clockwise or counter-clockwise allows you to adjust the tension or pressure of the snares as they lie across the bottom head.

11. *Snares* are wire, gut or plastic strands that stretch across the outside surface of the bottom head.

    a. Gut snares are made of catgut. They produce a dark, crisp and articulate sound, but are lacking in the ability to respond at softer dynamic levels. Like calfskin heads, they can be affected by weather and are commonly used in the marching field.

    b. Wire snares are made of coiled, spring-like strands. They have a bright sound and respond well at lower dynamic levels. As a result, they are the preferred choice of concert percussionists and drumset players.

    c. Plastic (nylon) snares are brighter than gut snares and are not affected by weather. They are articulate, and effective for marching use.

12. The *tone control* or *internal dampening knob* is mounted on the outside of the shell and attached to an internal muffler. When the knob is turned clockwise, the muffler presses against the batter head to absorb some of the vibrations and eliminate the after-ring.

REPLACING A DRUMHEAD

When Should a Drumhead Be Replaced?

Drumheads should be replaced immediately if torn or broken. They should also be replaced on a regular basis when the heads become worn. It is important to remember that the quality of sound continuously deteriorates as the drum is played; therefore, heads that are played loud and long (such as marching or heavy rock applications) will need to be changed more frequently than those played modestly and moderately (such as concert and/or jazz applications).

Materials Needed for Replacing a Drumhead

- new head
- drum key
- torque wrench (for marching drums)
- small box of paraffin wax (optional)
- jar of Vaseline
- damp rag and mild soap
- metal polish
- furniture polish
- flat-head or Phillips screwdriver (for removing the wire snares)
- can of WD-40
- hole-cutting template (optional)
- muffling materials (tape, gauze, foam, felt strips, pillow, etc.)

Drumhead Selection

The majority of today's drumheads are made of plastic or other synthetic material. Batter heads vary in thickness (thin, medium and thick) and may be either transparent or opaque. Though not affected by humidity, plastic heads can be affected by temperature, making them brittle during cold weather.

Calfskin heads, which were once used for all drums, remain available but are no longer popular due to price and maintenance factors. When used, they are more appropriate for larger drums (bass drum, timpani, etc.) used at the college or professional level.

Obtaining the Correct Drum Sound

Drumheads come in a variety of types, sizes, finishes and weights to accommodate the specific needs of drumset players in a variety of musical idioms (country, jazz, rock, pop, R&B, hip-hop, Latin, etc.). Each type of drumhead provides a specific sound, look and feel. The correct drum sound depends on a number of factors the player must be aware of, including the style of music being played and how drum sounds are used in different settings. For example, concert and jazz style drumming will generally require a medium-thick head, while marching and rock style drumming will typically require a thick head.

The following are some of the most common heads available on the market for drumset use.

Drumheads Available from Remo, Inc.

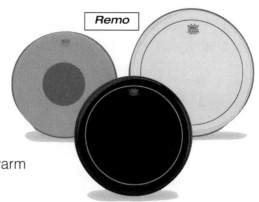

Renaissance   This head is the closest thing to calfskin. It features a textured surface that is excellent for sticks, brushes and mallets. It produces a warm and tonal sound.
Application: Great for melodic expression.
Sizes: Snare/Tom/Bass. *Finishes:* n/a.

Suede   Textured on both sides, this head combines the bright resonance and clarity of clear heads with the warm midrange articulation of coated WeatherKing heads.
Application: Great for all styles.
Sizes: Snare/Tom/Bass. *Finishes:* n/a.

Classic WeatherKing (Diplomat, Ambassador, Emperor)   This head is available in three standard finishes, from a bright-sounding clear head to a dark-sounding coated head. It produces a rich, full tone.
Application: Ideal for concert, jazz, rock and pop styles.
Sizes: Snare/Tom/Bass. *Finishes:* Coated, Clear.

PowerStroke 3 & 4   Contains a thin underlay ring at the outer edge of the head that subtly dampens unwanted overtones. It produces a full, deep tone.
Application: Ideal for the snare and bass drum, this head is good for all drumming styles and situations.
Sizes: Snare/Tom/Bass. *Finishes:* Coated, Clear, Renaissance; Suede (Bass only).

Smooth White   This head employs a unique film that creates a white look. It has excellent attack and sustain.
Application: Popular in rock and country styles.
Sizes: Snare/Tom/Bass. *Finishes:* Smooth White.

Ebony   With a classic look, this head produces a dark and resonant sound.
Application: Most often used as a front bass drum head.
Sizes: Snare/Tom/Bass. *Finishes:* Ebony series.

FiberSkyn 3   Created to simulate the characteristic look, sound and feel of drumheads in the jazz era, this head produces a dark, warm and round tone.
Application: Ideal for jazz, brushes, concert snare drums, bass drums and tom-toms.
Sizes: Snare/Tom/Bass. *Finishes:* n/a.

Controlled Sound   Combining medium and heavy-duty characteristics, this head features a Mylar dot (centered on either the top or bottom head) that eliminates high-frequency over-tones while adding durability and tonal focus.
Application: Ideal for the snare drum and heavy hitters.
Sizes: Snare/Tom/Bass. *Finishes:* Smooth White, Clear.

PinStripe   A two-ply head that features a ring-reducing agent between the plies of the outer edge of the stripe. The head produces a low-pitched sound with moderate attack and response characteristics and a quick decay.
Application: Ideal for the "fat" sounds of rock and R&B, and for creating a deeper, controlled sound in the studio and live situations.
Sizes: Snare/Tom/Bass. *Finishes:* Clear, Coated, Ebony.

Drumheads Available from Evans

EMAD (Externally Mounted Adjustable Damping)   This single-ply bass drum head consists of two interchangeable damping rings of varying width, giving the player the flexibility to fine-tune pedal response and muffling. The EMAD maximizes natural attack characteristics and offers tremendous low end and dynamic range.
Application: Great for all styles.
Sizes: 18–24. *Finishes:* Clear, Coated.

EQ Series   Featuring internal overtone control rings, removable muffle rings and dry vents, this series of single- and double-ply bass drum heads gives the player the ability to make small changes in setup and selection in order to achieve the ideal bass drum sound.
Application: Ideal for all styles. *Sizes:* 18–26. *Finishes:* Clear, Coated.

Evans

Power Center/Power Center Reverse Dot   Featuring a Power-Center Dot that adds durability and focus where the stick falls most, this single-ply snare head is especially good for hard hitters.   With the Power Center Reverse Dot, the dot has been moved to the underside of the head making it ideal for brush playing.
Application: Great for all styles. *Sizes:* 13–14. *Finishes:* Coated.

Genera   Similar to the EQ bass drum heads, this series for snare drum provides an extremely wide range of performance options. These heads feature dry vents and overtone control rings that allow players to dial up a graduated range of sounds.
Application: Ideal for all styles. *Sizes:* 12–14. *Finishes:* Coated.

J1 Etched   These single-ply tom and snare heads provide a big, wide-open and controlled drum sound. The "etching" process maximizes the sustain and frequency balance by making the film more flexible. This head combines the articulation of an uncoated head with the mellow warmth of a traditional coating. It has a natural earthiness that resembles traditional calfskin.
Application: Great for jazz, Latin and fusion styles. *Sizes:* 6–16. *Finishes:* Etched.

Genera G1   These single-ply tom and snare heads blend warmth, sustain and articulation. They are both durable and expressive.
Application: Jazz through light rock. *Sizes:* 6–20. *Finishes:* Clear, Coated.

Genera G2   These two-ply tom and snare heads offer the perfect blend of depth, sustain and attack. The coated heads provide extra control and roundness, while the clear heads provide a wide-open and bright attack.
Application: Light rock through heavy rock/pop styles.
Sizes: 6–20. *Finishes:* Clear, Coated.

Hydraulic   These heads contain a layer of oil between the plies that gives them a fat, wet sound. The oil acts as a natural muffler to decrease sustain and increase attack. These heads have a controlled, quick sustain.
Application: Best suited for rock and studio; also helpful for beginners who have difficulty tuning. *Sizes:* 6–20. *Finishes:* Glass (clear), Black, Blue.

THE SNARE DRUM

Changing the Drumhead

1. Determine the size of the drum by measuring from one side to the other, directly across the center. Do not include the hoop when measuring.

2. Select the proper replacement head, and check to make sure it is free from any defects, especially where the head enters the hoop.

3. Place the head, hoop down, onto a smooth countertop surface to see if it is straight.

4. Remove the tension rods, counterhoop and drumhead from your snare drum.

5. Clean the counterhoop and wipe the bearing edge of the shell clean. Wood and pearl finishes can be cleaned with a damp cloth and mild soap, and furniture polish may also be applied to wood finishes, if desired. Metal shells and hoops may be cleaned with a damp cloth and/or metal polish.

6. Before putting the new head in place, a thin coat of paraffin wax may be applied around the bearing edge of the drum shell (this is optional).

7. Set the new drumhead on the drum shell, and position it so the logo on the drumhead lines up with either the air hole or the drum shell logo.

8. Place the counterhoop over the drumhead, and carefully replace the tension rods after lubricating them with Vaseline or light machine oil. Using your fingers, systematically screw each tension rod in place and tighten them using only slight finger pressure. Before tuning, it will be helpful to number each tension rod using the snare release, logo or air hole as a point of reference for tension rod number 1.

Tuning the Snare Drum (Cross-Tension System)

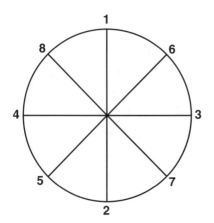

1. Tune the snare drum starting with the batter side. When incorporated into a drumset, the snare drum is usually tuned higher than the bass drum and tom-toms.

2. Starting with tension rod number 1, use a drum key or torque wrench (for marching drums) to tighten each rod one-half turn (or twist of the wrist). Do this repeatedly until the drumhead feels firm. Be sure not to tension any lug more than you do the others.

3. Once the initial tensioning of the drumhead is complete, you may get the head in tune with itself by *point tuning*. (Be sure to disengage the snares with the throw-off switch before beginning this step). Point tuning is achieved by tapping the head with a drumstick about two inches from each rod, to be certain the pitch is consistent all the way around the drum.

If it is not, adjust any location where the pitch is lower than average by turning the nearest tension rod clockwise as needed.

Adjust any location where the pitch is higher than average by turning the nearest tension rod counter-clockwise as needed.

Note: It is advisable to muffle the bottom head with something soft (like a pillow) while point tuning the top head, and vice versa. This will eliminate the problem of both heads resonating simultaneously, making it easier to point tune each individual head.

4. The procedure for tuning the snare head is the same as for the batter head, but with one additional step. Before changing the head, remove the snares on the bottom side of the drum. (It is only necessary to disconnect the snares from one end of the drum.)

5. Once the head has been replaced, reconnect the snares.

6. Tension the snare head firmly, but be sure that it is still able to vibrate freely against the snares. Some drummers tighten the batter head tighter than the snare, while others do the reverse. There is no firm rule; it is simply a matter of tone preference.

Tuning the Snare Drum (Clockwise System)

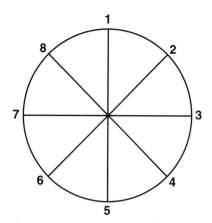

1. Starting with tension rod number 1, tighten each rod one twist of the wrist, moving sequentially around the drum in a circle.

2. Tap the head with a drumstick about two inches from each rod to be certain that the pitch is consistent all the way around the drum.

3. The procedure for tuning the snare head is the same as that for the batter head, but with one additional step. Before changing the head, remove the snares on the bottom side of the drum. (It is only necessary to disconnect the snares from one end of the drum.)

4. Once the head has been replaced, reconnect the snares.

5. Tension the snare head firmly, but be sure that it is still able to vibrate freely against the snares. Some drummers tighten the batter head tighter than the snare, while others do the reverse. There is no firm rule; it is simply a matter of tone preference.

Setting the Head

1. Once the head is in place and the correct tension has been achieved, take the palm of your hand and place it in the center of the drumhead.

2. Place your other hand on top and press firmly on the head with both hands. A cracking or popping sound is normal—it is simply the new head adjusting to the tension. Once this is done, the head will hold the tension consistently wherever you set it.

3. Make additional adjustments as needed.

Using the Snare Adjustment Screw

1. After achieving the desired pitch and tension for both heads, tap the batter head with a drumstick while adjusting the snare adjustment screw until the snares have been brought into contact with the snare head and the desired sound has been achieved.

2. Be careful not to over-tighten the drumheads or the snares, as you will choke the drum's sound. Remember that sound is produced by allowing the heads and snares to vibrate freely.

3. Test repeatedly by tapping the head lightly with a drumstick while making adjustments.

THE BASS DRUM

Drumset bass drum heads are referred to as the *front head* (audience side) and *back head* (player's side). Drumhead selection is made from a variety of combinations that may include coated, clear, pinstripe, black dot, etc. Again, head selection will be determined by the musical situation and the taste of the individual player.

front

back

Changing the Drumhead

1. Select the proper replacement head.

2. Remove the tension rods, counterhoop and drumhead from your bass drum.

3. Clean the counterhoop, and wipe the bearing edge of the shell clean. Wood and pearl finishes may be cleaned with a damp cloth and mild soap, and furniture polish may also be applied to wood finishes, if desired. Metal shells and hoops may be cleaned with a damp cloth and/or metal polish.

4. Before putting the new head in place, a thin coat of paraffin wax may be applied around the bearing edge of the drum shell (this is optional).

5. Set the new drumhead on the drum shell, and position it so the logo on the drumhead is at the top (photo A).

6. Place the counterhoop over the drumhead and carefully replace the tension rods after lubricating them with Vaseline or light machine oil. Using your fingers, screw each tension rod in place and tighten them using only slight finger pressure (photo B).

   Before tuning, it will be helpful to number each tension rod using either the logo or air hole as a point of reference for tension rod number 1 (photo C).

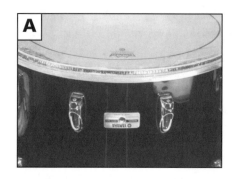

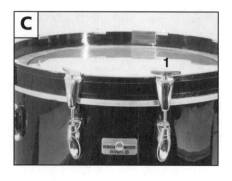

Tuning the Bass Drum (Cross-Tension System)

A solid, front bass drum head that is tuned properly with the batter head can provide a huge, punchy sound. When the heads are tuned up in pitch (such as in a jazz idiom), a very musical, resonant sound can be produced, something that works well with smaller bass drums.

1. Tune the head by using the cross-tension system of tuning as described for the snare drum on page 8.

2. When tuning the bass drum, use your fingers to turn two opposite rods from the base until all are snug, then begin cross tensioning at the top, one-half turn each (photo A). Continue this process until the desired pitch has been achieved. If the pitches are hard to hear, simply keep the amount of turns on each rod consistent. Higher tunings become more apparent.

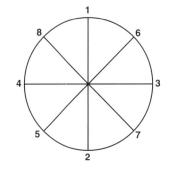

3. Once the initial tensioning of the drumhead is complete, get the head in tune with itself by point tuning. This is achieved by tapping the head with a drumstick about two inches from each rod to be certain that the pitch is consistent all the way around the drum (photo B). If it is not, adjust any location where the pitch is lower than average by turning the nearest tension rod clockwise as needed (photo C). Adjust any location where the pitch is higher than average by turning the nearest tension rod counter-clockwise as needed (photo D).

Note: It is advisable to muffle the bottom head with something soft (like a pillow) while point tuning the top head, and vice versa. This will eliminate the problem of both heads resonating simultaneously, making it easier to point tune each individual head.

Setting the Head

1. Once the head is in place and the correct tension has been applied, take the palm of your hand and place it in the center of the drumhead (photo E).

2. Place your other hand on top and press firmly on the head with both hands (photo F). A cracking or popping sound is normal—it is simply the new head adjusting to the tension. Once this is done, the head will hold the tension consistently wherever you set it.

3. Make additional adjustments as needed.

THE TOM-TOMS

Both heads of the drumset toms are batter heads, and are simply referred to as the top and bottom heads. As with the bass drum, both heads of a single drum do not have to be the same type, and head selection will again be determined by the musical situation and the individual player's taste.

Changing the Drumhead

1. Select the proper replacement head.

2. Remove the tension rods, counterhoop and drumhead from your tom-tom.

3. Wipe the bearing edge of the shell clean. Wood and pearl finishes may be cleaned with a damp cloth and mild soap, and furniture polish may also be applied to wood finishes, if desired. Metal shells and hoops may be cleaned with a damp cloth and/or metal polish.

4. Before putting the new head in place, a thin coat of paraffin wax may be applied around the bearing edge of the drum shell (this is optional).

5. Set the new drumhead on the drum shell and position it so the logo on the drumhead lines up with either the air hole or the drum shell logo (photo A).

6. Place the counterhoop over the drumhead and carefully replace the tension rods after lubricating them with Vaseline or light machine oil. Using your fingers, screw each tension rod in place and tighten them using only slight finger pressure (photo B).

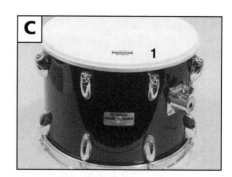

Before tuning, it will be helpful to number each tension rod using either the logo or air hole as a point of reference for tension rod number 1 (photo C).

Tuning the Tom-Toms
(Cross-Tension System)

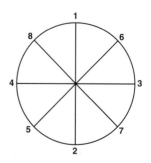

1. Tune the head by using the cross-tension system of tuning as described for the snare drum on page 8.

2. It is important that the tension be equalized around the entire circumference of the tom-tom to obtain the best tone. Again, this is accomplished in much the same manner as for the snare drum.

3. Once the initial tensioning of the drumhead is complete, get the head in tune with itself by point tuning. This is achieved by tapping the head with a drumstick about two inches from each rod to be certain that the pitch is consistent all the way around the drum (photo A).

   If it is not, adjust any location where the pitch is lower than average by turning the nearest tension rod clockwise as needed (photo B).

   Adjust any location where the pitch is higher than average by turning the nearest tension rod counter-clockwise as needed (photo C).

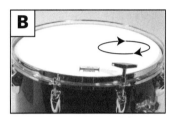 

Note: It is advisable to muffle the bottom head with something soft (like a pillow) while point tuning the top head, and vice versa. This will eliminate the problem of both heads resonating simultaneously, making it easier to point tune each individual head.

Tuning Multiple Toms

Multiple tom-toms of varied diameters should be tuned from high to low as one moves from left to right. Some players prefer tuning the three tom-toms of a standard five-piece set using a triad[1] (from low to high tom) with the bass drum tuned to a fourth[2] below the low tom (also called the *floor tom*).

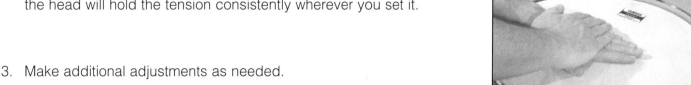

Setting the Head

1. Once the head is in place and the correct tension has been achieved, take the palm of your hand and place it in the center of the drumhead.

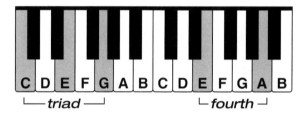

2. Place your other hand on top and press firmly on the head with both hands. A cracking or popping sound is normal—it is simply the new head adjusting to the new tension. Once this is done, the head will hold the tension consistently wherever you set it.

3. Make additional adjustments as needed.

[1] A *triad* is a three-note chord consisting of a root, third and fifth (for example, C–E–G).

[2] A *fourth* is an interval consisting of five half steps, or the interval between the first and fourth notes of a major or minor scale (for example, E up to A).

MUFFLING

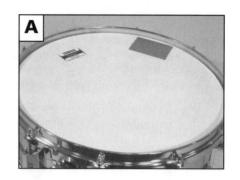

In various musical or studio situations, a certain amount of ring or harmonic overtones may need to be removed from the sound. In order to reduce the desired amount of head resonance, drums can be muffled in a variety of ways, including placing tape, gauze, foam or other materials on the surface of the drumhead. It is important to remember that placing any material on the head will reduce the resonance and projection of the drum.

Several drum companies manufacture effective muffling systems such as the Evans EQ and RGS (Resonance Gate System) Pads, the Min-EMAD, the Remo Muffls and the DW Drum Pillow. Each of these systems will provide adequate and adjustable muffling.

Muffling the Snare Drum

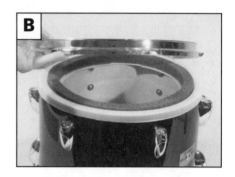

1. The desired balance of dampening and resonance may be achieved by selecting the right type of head.

2. If more dampening is desired, additional muffling can be achieved by placing a small amount of duct tape or piece of cloth to the top exterior of the batter head, near the edge (photo A).

3. The use of the internal muffler included on some models is not recommended, as it muffles the head by applying pressure from the underside of the head, restricting the natural resonance of the drum.

Muffling the Tom-Toms

1. The desired balance of dampening and resonance may be achieved by selecting the right type of head.

2. If more dampening is desired, the tom-toms can be muffled by placing tape, gauze or other materials on the surface of the head as needed to remove the desired amount of harmonics or ring from the sound (photos A and B). Doing so, however, will reduce a certain amount of resonance, which may affect the projection of the drum.

Muffling the Bass Drum

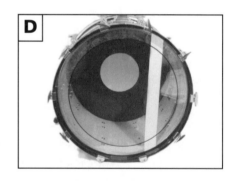

1. The desired balance of dampening and resonance may be achieved by selecting the right type of head.

2. Felt strips may be placed behind both heads of the bass drum, and some players may choose to place a pillow, blanket or piece of foam rubber inside the drum. In this case, the cost is minimal, and the sound can be customized to fit your needs (photos C and D).

   Keep in mind, however, that while this effectively muffles the drum, it also produces a sound that lacks resonance, making the timbre of this drum different from that of the other drums in the set.

3. Front bass drum heads may also be purchased either with a six-inch hole cut off-center, or with a larger center hole. (If you would like to cut your own hole, the use of a hole-cutting template will allow you to choose your own placement.) The front hole allows air to escape, resulting in a more direct sound while retaining some of the resonant qualities of the front head. It also allows a microphone to be placed inside the drum at varying degrees (photo E).

PART 2 HOW TO SET UP YOUR DRUMSET

Since the inception of the drumset at the turn of the 20th century, the primary role of the drumset player has been that of an accompanist, functioning not only as the metronome or time keeper, but also as the creator of basic beats and patterns from which playing is based within various styles.

Over the years, the components of the "standard" drumset have changed as musical styles and tastes have evolved. For example, during the 1940s and 1950s, the standard drumset consisted of four drums (snare, bass, a mounted tom and floor tom), a ride cymbal, crash cymbal, pair of hi-hat cymbals, and perhaps some accessory instruments such as a cowbell and woodblock. With the evolution of rock 'n' roll, pop, etc., the cowbell and woodblock were replaced by an additional tom, making the standard drumset a five-piece setup rather than a four-piece setup.

During the 1960s and 1970s, the size of the drumset increased considerably with the addition of multiple toms, a second bass drum, specialty cymbals (sizzle, Chinese, splash, etc.), and even more accessory instruments (wind chimes, roto-toms, electronic trigger pads, etc.).

Today, a "standard" drumset is a four- or five-piece setup containing the four basic elements: drums, cymbals, hardware (stands, mounting devices and pedals) and throne. A standard five-piece set includes a snare drum, bass drum (with a bass drum pedal), two mounted tom-toms (with mounting hardware), a floor tom-tom, cymbals (with stands), a hi-hat stand and a drum throne. As mentioned above, additional drums, including an additional bass drum, cymbals and accessory instruments, may be added to the basic setup.

THE OVERALL SETUP

The drums and cymbals should be centralized around the player in such a way as to minimize reaching, stretching and twisting. The drums should be set up to accommodate the player—not the reverse.

Comfortable positioning of the drumset and a relaxed approach will help to facilitate smooth motion. The type of motion employed in playing will be reflected in the quality of sound. Relaxed motions will produce smooth, controlled sounds, while stiff motions will produce tight, constrained sounds. It is important that you strive for a relaxed approach.

ARRANGING THE DRUMS

The Snare Drum

A standard snare drum is 14 inches in diameter.
Some drummers may also use a 13-inch piccolo snare drum.

Piccolo Snare Drum

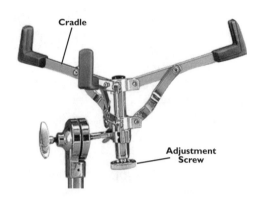

The components of the snare drum are the shell (made of either wood, metal or fiberglass), two counterhoops (rims), lugs and tension rods (the number of which depends on the size of the drum), a snare head and a batter head, a snare strainer (which includes a throw-off switch/snare adjustment screw), a muffler (operated by an internal dampening knob), and the snares (made of either wire, nylon or gut). See photo on page 4.

1. The drum is placed on top of a stand, referred to as the *cradle*. Once securely in the cradle, a screw at the bottom of the cradle allows the stand to be tightened around the circumference of the drum. Be careful not to overtighten the screw as this may choke the sound of the drum.

2. The height of the stand may be adjusted to fit the player's needs.

3. The drum should be placed to the right of the hi-hat (for a right-handed player) and rotated so that the throw-off switch is easily accessible.

4. Whether played with matched or traditional grip, the snare drum should be positioned and angled so that the proper alignment of the forearms and hands is not affected.

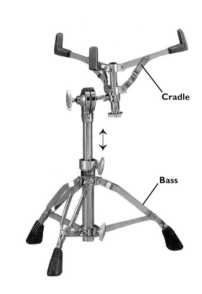

- With **matched grip,** the snare drum is usually flat or slanted slightly downward and toward the player.

- With **traditional grip,** the snare drum is usually tilted slightly downward and (if right-handed) to the right.

The Bass Drum

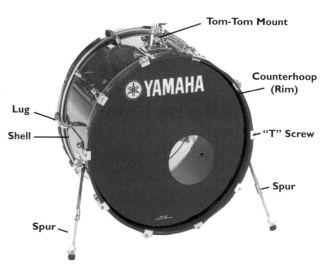

The bass drum, also referred to as the *kick drum,* is usually between 18 and 26 inches in diameter, 22 inches being the most common. It may have one or two heads. A second bass drum may be added to the basic five-piece setup.

The components of the bass drum are the shell (made of either wood or fiberglass), two counterhoops (rims), lugs and tension rods (the number of which depends on the size of the drum), a tom-tom mount (for either one or two tom-toms), one or two heads, and two spurs (one attached to each side) to keep the drum from tilting side to side or sliding forward (see photo).

The use of a rug or mat is strongly recommended as it will not only protect floors and the bottom of the drum, but will also help keep the drum from sliding forward as it is being played.

The Bass Drum Pedal and Pedal Tension Adjustment

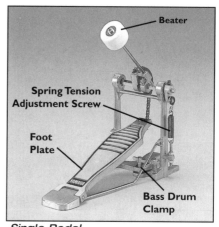

Single Pedal

1. The bass drum is played with a single or double bass drum pedal, clamped to the rim of the bass drum and operated by the foot. In addition to the foot plate, it consists of a beater and a spring tension adjustment screw.

2. Various types of beaters are available for the bass drum pedal. The following are brief descriptions of the main beater types.

    *   **Medium Felt Beater** This is a good, general-purpose beater capable of producing a medium punch or fatter attack. It is denser than the large felt beater, and is good for medium-volume music.

    *   **Large Felt Beater** This beater is larger than a medium felt beater, and less dense. It is primarily used to produce a tone that is deeper in timbre, but not usually one with a loud punch or attack.

    *   **Rubber Beater** Because this beater is more dense than one made of felt, it will deliver a stronger punch. It will not, however, produce as much punch or attack as one made of plastic or wood.

    *   **Wood/Plastic Beater** Beaters made of plastic or wood are very dense and heavy. They are capable of producing very powerful and sharp attacks, and are especially good for rock and Latin applications.

    *   **Two-Way Beater** A good combination of felt on one side and hard plastic on the other, this beater can produce both tones of felt and wood. Because the plastic side is similar to wood, it is capable of producing a very powerful and sharp attack. This beater is used in a variety of musical styles because of its versatility.

3. After the beater strikes the drumhead, the spring returns the beater to its original position unless the return stroke has been restricted by pressing the beater against the head.

4. Adjust the pedal's spring tension to offer firm resistance to the action of the foot pedal. The tighter the tension, the faster the rebound of the pedal.

5. Two fundamental techniques for playing the bass drum are *heel up* and *heel down*.

- When using the **heel down** technique, the entire foot contacts the pedal. The player rocks the foot with an ankle motion, causing the beater to strike the head. The foot then returns immediately to the "up" position, without leaving the pedal as shown in photos A and B.

- When using the **heel up** technique (often used for louder, more articulate strokes), the heel is raised one to two inches off the pedal surface, while the ball of the foot operates the pedal. The foot returns immediately to the "up" position as shown in photos C and D. For greater volume, the leg may be used in conjunction with the ankle.

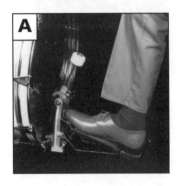
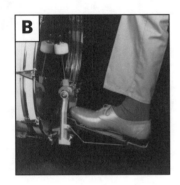

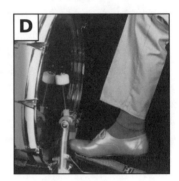

The Mounted (Rack) Tom-Toms

One or more mounted toms may be used, ranging in size from 6 to18 inches in diameter, 12 or 13 inches being the most common.

"Power" drum sizes are also available, which extend the depth of the shell to create a lower pitch and darker sound than that of the traditional tom-tom. These particular drums may increase the overall volume and height of the drumset because of the extended length of the tom-toms mounted on the bass drum.

The components of the tom-tom are the shell (made of either wood or fiberglass), two counterhoops (rims), lugs and tension rods (the number of which depends on the size of the drum), one or two heads, and a mount attached to the side of the drum to secure it to the top of the bass drum.

1. The tom-toms should be tuned before attaching them to the bass drum, as it will become more difficult to do so once they've been put in place. (See page 14 for a complete explanation.)

2. Attach the tom-toms to the mount on top of the bass drum, making sure they don't touch or rub against the bass drum, snare drum or floor tom. Tilt the drums slightly toward you in such a way that you clear the rims while striking the heads comfortably with the side of the stick tip (see photo). Avoiding a severe drumstick angle will not only produce the best tone, but will also reduce the likelihood of damaging the drumhead. If using more than one mounted tom, large gaps in height between the batter heads of the drums should be avoided, as well as large distances between each drum.

The Floor Tom-Tom

The largest of the tom-toms, the floor tom, usually ranges in size from 14 to 16 inches in diameter, 16 inches being the most common. It may have one or two heads.

The components of the floor tom-tom are the shell (made of either wood or fiberglass), two counterhoops (rims), lugs and tension rods (the number of which depends on the size of the drum), and three legs (or a stand with mount) that can be adjusted to fit your needs.

1. Place the floor tom to the right of the snare drum (for a right-handed player) at approximately the same height. It may be angled slightly toward you or toward the snare drum.

2. When more than one floor tom-tom is used, large gaps in height between the batter heads of the drums should be avoided, as well as large distances between each drum.

The Drum Throne

The position and height of the drum throne is critical to proper balance, and directly affects the flexibility and performance of the feet. Because each person is built differently, throne adjustments are of a personal nature (as are most drumset positions). It is crucial, however, to find a height and distance that will allow total relaxation, specifically of the hips, legs, ankles and upper body. If you experience pain in your lower back, additional adjustments will need to be made.

1. Adjust the throne height so the hip is slightly above the knee when sitting.

2. Draw an imaginary straight line vertically from the front of your knee to the back of your foot. In this position, the ligaments, tendons and muscles are flexible and free to move naturally whether you play heel up or heel down. (Stretching exercises will help achieve maximum flexibility.)

3. From this position, make slight height and distance adjustments to suit your own personal needs. Remember that if you sit too close or far away from the drumset, your limbs may move unnaturally and cause undo stress on your joints, ligaments and muscles. This, in turn, will minimize flexibility when playing. Remember—always set the drums up to *you!*

ARRANGING DRUMSET CYMBALS

The standard cymbal setup will include a ride cymbal, one or two crash cymbals and a pair of hi-hat cymbals. Most drummers will have at least two crash cymbals before adding additional specialty cymbals to their setup.

If you are using several cymbals, it is wise to arrange them around yourself in such a way as to minimize reaching, stretching and twisting. The exact placement, of course, will depend on your physical size and technical ability. Proper cymbal positioning will help to assure optimum sound quality and volume while minimizing the possibility of damage to the cymbal.

The Hi-Hat

The hi-hat (sometimes called the *sock cymbal*) consists of a pair of cymbals, usually 14 to 15 inches in diameter, mounted "facing" one above the other. The most popular combination of hi-hat cymbals is a medium-thin top cymbal and a medium or medium-heavy bottom cymbal.

1. The cymbals are placed on a special stand that includes an adjustable tension spring in its shaft (see photo), and a foot pedal attached to a rod. When the pedal is pressed, the top cymbal is lowered onto the bottom one.

2. The bottom cymbal rests on top of a felt-covered platform. The top cymbal is held by felt pads and a special mounting bracket called a *clutch*. The clutch is attached to a rod that moves up and down with the pedal. When at rest, the space between the two cymbals should be approximately 1 to 2 inches.

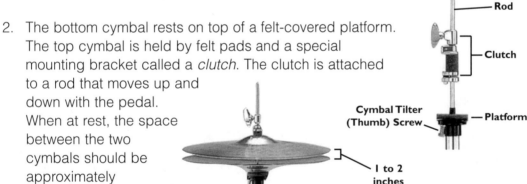

3. The hi-hat should be placed to the left of (and slightly higher than) the snare drum, and operated (by a right-handed player) with the left foot.

4. When the foot pedal is pressed, the cymbals are brought together to produce a crisp, "chick" sound. (Note: If the cymbals are perfectly parallel to one another, no sound will result. Use the thumb screw located beneath the bottom cymbal to tilt it slightly, thereby producing the distinctive "chick" sound.)

5. The hi-hat spring's tension should be adjusted to offer firm resistance to the foot pedal's action. The tighter the tension, the faster the rebound of the pedal.

6. Two fundamental techniques for playing the hi-hat are *heel-toe (rocking)* and *toe.*

- The **heel-toe** or **rocking** technique is often used when playing repetitive strokes on beats 2 and 4. As the ball of the foot presses the pedal down on beats 2 and 4, the heel rises off the pedal; on beats 1 and 3, the ball of the foot rises as the heel goes back down (photos A and B).

- The **toe** technique is particularly useful for executing rapid or unusual rhythms. When using this technique, the leg is raised to lift the heel from the pedal while the ball of the foot is bounced up and down to activate the hi-hat. Keep your leg relaxed and ankle flexible so the foot feels like it is being bounced rather than lifted up by the leg (photos C and D).

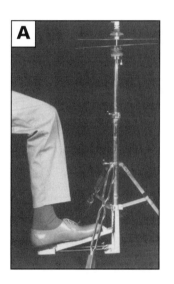  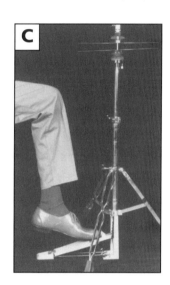 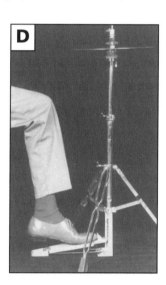

Playing on the Hi-Hat

1. As an alternative to the ride cymbal, the hi-hat can be played with a drumstick (using the tip or shoulder) to strike the top hi-hat cymbal, creating an articulate, ostinato effect. This is particularly effective in rock and Latin styles.

2. The hi-hat may also be played while the cymbals are open, partially closed (cymbals lightly touching to provide a looser, "swishing" sound) or completely closed. A plus (+) sign represents a closed hi-hat; an open hi-hat is designated by a letter o (o). Accented notes may be produced by striking the edge of the hi-hat with the shoulder of the stick. Non-accented notes are produced by striking the top of the hi-hat (not the bell) with the tip of the stick.

Additional Hi-Hat Cymbal Types

Aside from the basic hi-hat setup described above, there are varieties of specialized hi-hat cymbals available that can produce a wide range of sounds. Some of these additional cymbal types include flat, sizzle and rippled-edge hi-hats.

Flat

Sizzle

Rippled-Edge

The Ride Cymbal

The function of the ride cymbal is to maintain an ostinato beat or pattern. Because greater volume and projection is required, ride cymbals are generally thicker and larger than other cymbal types.

A ride cymbal is usually 18 to 22 inches in diameter, and medium to medium-heavy in weight. It should be positioned in such a way as to allow the stick to strike 2 to 4 inches in from the edge. You should not have to extend your upper arm from its natural hanging position in order to reach the playing areas of the cymbal.

1. The ride cymbal should be mounted on a cymbal stand, supported by a metal washer covered with felt (see photo). The threaded tube should be sheathed in a piece of rubber or nylon tubing. A felt pad should be placed on top of the cymbal so that the wing nut does not make contact with the cymbal (this would not only restrict the cymbal's sound, but may also cause the cymbal to crack as it vibrates widely on its axis).

2. Boom stands are also available and may be used for larger, heavier cymbals, offering greater flexibility when positioning them.

Playing the Ride Cymbal

The three main areas of the cymbal are the *edge, profile* or *bow,* and *bell* or *dome.*

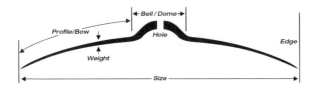

1. The ride cymbal may be struck in a variety of places to obtain different sounds. When it is struck on the bell, it will produce a high-pitched "ping" sound, effective for Latin-American rhythms or "funk" (photos A and B).

2. When struck near the edge, a ride cymbal will produce a broad sound with prominent midrange overtones.

3. About 2 to 4 inches in from the edge is considered the best area for playing the ride-cymbal pattern (photo C). The exact sound, however, is a matter of personal taste and preference.

4. A variety of interesting effects can be created by using the tip, shoulder and butt end of the drumstick on the ride cymbal.

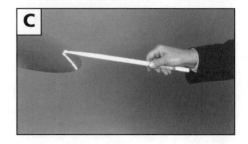

5. Excessive ringing of a ride cymbal may be eliminated by placing two small strips of tape on the cymbal's underside (perhaps also to each side of the cymbal bell as shown in the following diagram). This is particularly effective when more definition and clarity is required, such as in a live room or in a recording studio. Obviously, tape may be removed when necessary without harming the cymbal.

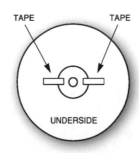

The Crash Cymbal

The function of the crash cymbal is to punctuate, accent or reinforce a sudden "explosive" sound rather than to execute a particular rhythm. Because a quick attack and decay is required of this cymbal, it is generally thinner and smaller than a ride cymbal.

One or more crash cymbals may be used so that a cymbal can be matched with a particular sound. Crash cymbals usually range from 16 to 18 inches in diameter, and are from thin to medium in weight.

1. Crash cymbals are generally tilted slightly and positioned within normal reach so as to allow the drumstick's shaft to strike the cymbal's bow and/or edge at a 45-degree angle (see photo below).

Some drummers place their crash cymbals above normal playing height to maximize visual effect.

2. Extreme angling of a crash cymbal will restrict the cymbal's movement, diminish its response and put unnecessary pressure on the bell (cup) area. If a greater cymbal angle is desired, a cymbal tilter—often using a spring as a shock absorber—may be useful.

Playing the Crash Cymbal

1. It is suggested that you use a quick blow and follow-through when striking a crash cymbal.

2. Never overplay a cymbal in order to produce more volume. If more power is needed, you should seek larger, heavier cymbals, which are not as likely to break during loud playing.

Choking the Crash Cymbal

Sometimes, it is desirable to shorten the after-ring of a crash cymbal. This is done by grabbing the cymbal's edge with the free hand as shown below.

Although this effect is more frequently applied to crash cymbals, it may be employed on cymbals of all types and in any setting, as needed.

Additional Cymbal Types

Aside from the basic cymbal setup described above, many varieties of specialized cymbals are available that can produce a wide range of sounds and sometimes visual effects. These cymbals come in a wide range of sizes, shapes, colors, weights and sound characteristics, and are frequently used by drummers to supplement their basic cymbal setup. Some of these additional cymbal types include sizzle, splash, Chinese, octagonal, flat-bell, minibell, megabell, flange-ride, grooveless, and cymbals with a colored finish.

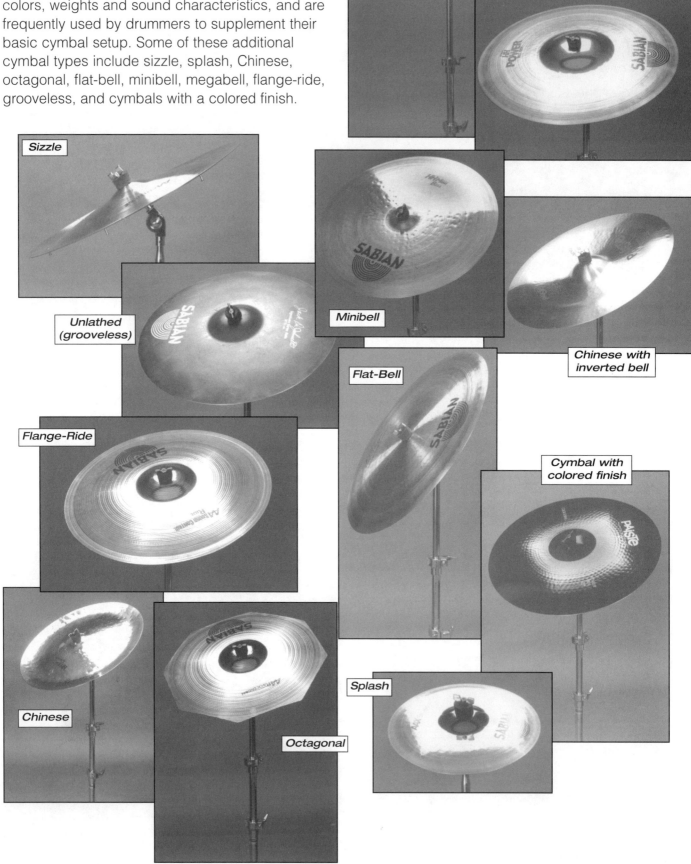

Chinese (turned upside down)

Megabell

Sizzle

Minibell

Unlathed (grooveless)

Chinese with inverted bell

Flat-Bell

Flange-Ride

Cymbal with colored finish

Chinese

Octagonal

Splash

CHOOSING DRUMSTICKS AND MALLETS

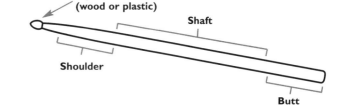

Tip or Bead
(wood or plastic)

Shaft

Shoulder

Butt

Snare Drum Sticks

The parts of the drumstick are the *butt end, shaft, shoulder,* and *bead* or *tip.*

Snare drum sticks are most often made of wood (usually maple, oak or hickory). Plastic, fiberglass and metal have also been tried, but with limited success.

1. Drumsticks come in a variety of sizes and shapes, designed for different sounds and/or applications. A stick with a small tip is articulate, whereas one with a larger, rounder tip produces a broad, full sound.

2. Sticks are available with either a wood or a nylon tip. Those with nylon tips are designed to produce a more articulated sound on the cymbals (especially useful for a repeating ostinato pattern). When used on a drum, however, they sound almost identical to a wood-tipped stick.

3. "A" model sticks (originally designed for jazz playing) are smaller than "B" model sticks (designed for heavier use in a concert band), which are smaller than "S" model sticks (intended for street or marching use), which are smaller than "DC" sticks (designed for drum-corp use).

4. For beginning snare drummers, a "2B" or "5B" model stick is recommended. For those playing in a jazz or concert band setting, a "5A" or "5B" drumstick is a good, standard stick to start with. For those playing in a rock or heavy metal band, a larger pair of sticks may be desired. Whatever your choice, you should always carry multiple pairs in the event they break or get lost.

5. When purchasing sticks, it is recommended that you check them carefully to make sure you're buying a matched pair. The following guidelines will help you make that determination:

   a. Visually inspect each stick for obvious flaws.

   b. Tap each stick on a hard surface and listen for an even match. Sticks that produce a high pitch are most likely made of dense wood, which is excellent for both sound and response.

   c. Check to make sure the sticks are not warped by rolling each one on a hard, flat surface. Those that are warped should be discarded.

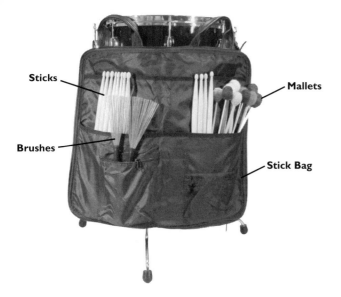

Sticks

Brushes

Mallets

Stick Bag

Brushes and Mallets

1. Because brushes produce the second most-requested sound, every drummer should carry at least one pair. Brushes can be made of wire or nylon, be retractable or non-retractable, and have handles made of wood, plastic or metal. Like sticks, they come in a variety of sizes and weights.

2. Any of the various types of mallets covered with yarn or felt are recommended for use on the tom-toms (good for soft, muted sounds) or for suspended cymbal rolls.

A stick bag is recommended for the storage and transportation of your sticks, mallets and brushes. They come in a variety of sizes, styles, colors and materials, and can be attached to the side of the floor tom-tom for easy access while playing.

READY TO PLAY:
PRACTICE TIPS TO MAKE THE MOST OF YOUR DRUMSET

- Make sure your equipment is working for you and not against you. If you're experiencing pain while practicing/playing, look into the reason why and make the necessary fixes and/or adjustments.

- Spend time warming up at the beginning of each practice session to get the blood flowing and the body functioning smoothly and efficiently. Non-musical warm-ups may include walking, running or a variety of calisthenics.

- One of the most important roles of a drummer is to keep good time. Learning to practice with either a metronome (preferably one with a headphone output), a drum machine, or a computer with music sequencing software will help you to achieve this.

- Start slowly. Practice each rhythm or exercise at a comfortable, consistent tempo before increasing the speed.

- Count aloud, and either clap or sing each rhythm before playing. Don't move on until you can play what you're practicing at an equal volume and tempo throughout.

- Maintain a relaxed feel while playing, and breathe normally (breathing and relaxation are very crucial elements of drumming).

- Strive to get the best tone out of your drums and cymbals.

- Strive for proper balance. Are all the notes even and in consistent time? Are the parts of the drumset balanced dynamically?

- As you practice, use a mirror to observe your hands, arms, legs, feet, stick height and posture.

- Try to look for any bad habits (your teacher or your own observations should point these out).

- Focus! When concentrating fully, things become more ingrained in your mind, making them easier to recall later.

- Experiment with rhythms and patterns that *you* create.

- Set new goals for yourself.

- Consistent practice is important in order to keep your body in good condition and to get the most out of your practice sessions.

- Actively listen to a variety of musical styles, as this is one of the best learning tools available.

- Keep a practice diary.

- Enjoy practicing. Playing drums is fun, and regular practice sessions will make you a better player.

- Always practice and play musically.

PART 3 CARE AND MAINTENANCE

Proper care, storage and regular maintenance of your equipment will yield positive results for years to come.

DRUMS

Cases and Storage

1. When your drumset remains set up but is not being used, keep it covered with an old, but clean, sheet or blanket to protect it from dust and dirt.

2. When your drumset is not in use for longer periods of time, place the drums in cases and store them where they are not subjected to either extreme cold or heat.

3. When transporting your drums and hardware, it is strongly recommended that you use any number of commercially available cases (either leather, canvas, nylon or fiber) designed specifically for the storage and transport of drums and hardware.

Drumheads

Drumheads should be kept free from dirt and replaced when they become worn or broken. They may be cleaned with mild soap and water (though this is not common practice). Do not allow moisture to accumulate between the edge of the head and the counterhoop.

Drum Shells

Regular cleaning of your drums will help prolong their beauty and tone. Wood and pearl finishes may be cleaned with a damp cloth and mild soap; furniture polish may also be applied to wood finishes, if desired. Shells should be checked periodically for cracks.

Hardware

Lugs should be checked to make sure they are tightly secured to the shell. Tension rods should be lubricated with Vaseline or light grease. Those that are bent or stripped should be replaced. Moving parts, including the snare throw-off switch, bass drum pedal and hi-hat pedal, should be lubricated once or twice a year with light machine oil.

Metal shells and hoops may be cleaned with a damp cloth and/or metal polish. Broken snares, warped rims, and faulty strainers should be fixed or replaced immediately.

CYMBALS

Storage and Shipment

1. Cymbals should not be stored where they will be subject to either extreme cold or heat, as a temporary loss of sound may occur until normal temperature has been restored.

2. When transporting cymbals, it is suggested that you use a leather, canvas or nylon padded bag made specifically for cymbals. There are also fiber cases specifically designed for cymbal transport.

3. Bass drum and trap cases sometimes have special compartments for the specific purpose of carrying cymbals. If more than one cymbal is being carried or stored in a single bag or case, it is suggested that padding be used to separate the cymbals to prevent scratching.

Cleaning Cymbals

1. Fingerprints and dirt can be removed by using a solution of mild liquid dishwater detergent and warm water. Most cymbal manufacturers market specially formulated cymbal-cleaning products as well. If further cleaning becomes necessary, there are a number of nonabrasive commercial cleansers available on the market.

2. Never use steel wool, wire brushes or any other abrasive cleanser. If a cymbal is exceptionally old and dirty, a stiff fiber brush may be used. Never use an electric buffing device, as the heat generated will alter a cymbal's temper, making it vulnerable to cracking.

3. Cymbal felts and plastic sleeves on cymbal stands should be checked on a regular basis to make sure that the cymbal is not making contact with the stand, which will not only restrict the cymbal's sound, but may also cause the cymbal to crack.

Repairing Cymbal Cracks

1. Even with proper care and maintenance, cymbals can still develop cracks. If a crack occurs, it must be eliminated as soon as possible because eventually the smallest nick will develop into a large crack. For cracks that start from the outer edge and move inward, an eighth-inch hole may be drilled just ahead of the crack (diagram A). For cracks that appear horizontally across the bow of the cymbal, an eighth-inch hole should be drilled on both ends of the crack. Cracks up to about one-half inch that appear on the edge of the cymbal can be ground out (diagram B).

2. Never attempt to braze or weld cymbals, as the heat will cause irreversible damage.

3. It is important to remember that these techniques have been proven successful in stopping cracks from spreading, but there is no guarantee they will work in all cases, or indefinitely.

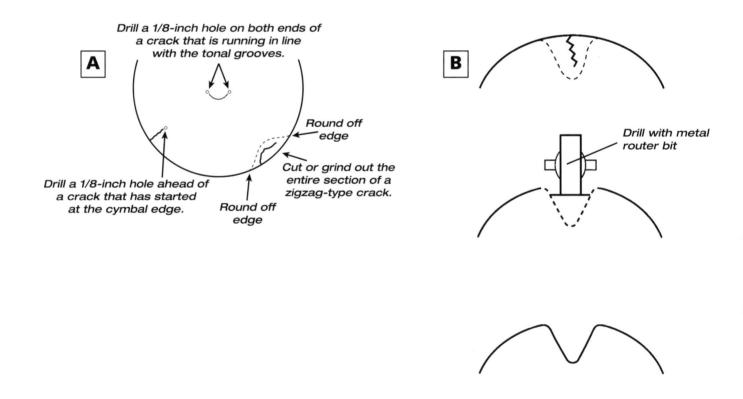

GLOSSARY OF DRUMMING TERMS

accent: To emphasize a note; indicated by a > symbol.

after-ring: The ringing of a drum or cymbal as it continues to resonate after being struck.

air vent: A hole in the side of the drum shell that allows air to escape when the batter head is struck.

articulate: To strike a drum or cymbal in a particular manner to obtain a specific sound.

attack: The manner in which you begin a note.

bass drum pedal: Clamped to the rim of the bass drum and operated by the foot.

batter head: The top head of the snare drum or tom-tom, or the front head of the bass drum.

bead (or **tip**): The front part of the drumstick used to strike the drum or cymbal.

bearing edge: The point on the drum where the head meets the rim.

bell (or **dome**): The top (center) part of the cymbal.

bow (or **profile**): The area of the cymbal between the edge and bell.

brushes: Devices made of wire or nylon, used to strike or sweep a drumhead or cymbal.

butt end: The back part of a drumstick.

calfskin head: The skin of a calf stretched over one or both ends of a drum and struck with a hand, mallet or stick.

cases: Used to store and/or transport drums, cymbals and accessories.

chick sound: The sound produced by the hi-hat cymbals when the foot pedal is pressed and the cymbals are brought together.

clamp: A device used to attach the bass drum pedal to the rim of the bass drum.

clockwise system: A method of tuning carried out by moving sequentially around the drum, as opposed to the cross-tension system.

clutch: A mounting bracket used to hold the top hi-hat cymbal to the rod of the hi-hat stand.

counterhoop (or **rim**): Used to hold the drumhead in place.

cradle: The top part of the stand that holds the drum.

crisp sound: Sharp, clean and clear.

cross-tension system: A method of tuning carried out by moving cross-wise around the drum, as opposed to the clockwise system.

cymbal tilter screw (or **thumb screw**): Used to tilt the bottom hi-hat cymbal that sits on the platform.

dark sound: Possessing depth and richness.

decay: The gradual fading out of a sound.

dome (or **bell**): The top (center) part of the cymbal.

drumhead: The material (plastic or skin) stretched over one or both ends of a drum and struck with a hand, mallet or stick.

drum key: A key used to tighten or loosen the tension rods for the purpose of tuning or removing drumheads.

drumstick: A stick used to strike a drum or cymbal, consisting of a tip (or bead), shoulder, shaft, and butt end.

drum throne: What a drummer sits on when playing.

dynamics: Varying degrees of volume.

edge: The outer part of the cymbal.

explosive sound: Giant and sudden.

fatter attack: Full and rich.

felt strip: A piece of material used to muffle the sound of a drum; may be placed behind both heads of the bass drum.

flesh hoop: A wooden or metal ring to which the head is attached by means of glue or pressure.

foot plate: A plate on which the foot operating the bass drum pedal or hi-hat pedal rests.

harmonic overtones: High pitches that resonate after a drum or cymbal has been struck.

heel-toe technique: A technique of playing the bass drum and hi-hat by which the entire foot contacts the pedal.

hi-hat pedal: Operated by the foot; brings the hi-hat cymbals together when pressed.

hole-cutting template: A pattern or mold used as a guide for cutting a hole in the bass drum head.

internal dampening knob: Mounted on the outside of the shell and attached to the internal muffler; when turned clockwise, the muffler presses against the batter head.

internal muffler: When pressed against the batter head, it absorbs some of the vibrations and eliminates the after-ring or resonance.

kick drum: Another name for the bass drum.

lugs: Attached to the side of the drum and used as receptacles for the tension rods.

mallets: Sticks with a yarn or felt-covered ball at the end, used to strike a drum or produce suspended cymbal rolls.

matched grip: Both hands hold a drumstick or mallet in the same manner (with palms down).

muffler: A device used to absorb vibrations and eliminate after-ring.

muffling: A technique used to reduce head resonance, ring, or harmonic overtones.

muted: Softened or muffled.

opaque drumhead: A solid-colored drumhead.

ostinato: An accompaniment pattern that is repeated.

pitch: The location of a note in terms of its highness or lowness.

platform: The piece of the hi-hat stand upon which the bottom cymbal sits.

point tuning: A means of checking to make sure the pitch is consistent all the way around the drum.

profile (or **bow**): The area of a cymbal between the edge and bell.

punch: With a quick, sudden blow or attack.

resonance: A ringing or long decay.

rim (or **counterhoop**): Used to hold a drumhead in place.

ring: A resonant tone.

rod: A part of the hi-hat stand to which the top cymbal is attached via the clutch.

setting the head: A procedure used to hold the tension of the head consistently wherever you set it.

shaft: The middle part of a drumstick between the shoulder and butt end.

shell: The frame that supports all the other components of the drum.

shoulder: The area of a drumstick between the tip (bead) and the shaft.

snare head: The bottom head of a snare drum.

snare release (or **snare strainer**): Attached to the side of the snare drum, used to engage or disengage the snares from the snare head by means of a throw-off switch.

snares: Wire, nylon or gut strands stretched across the outside surface of the snare head.

snare strainer: See **snare release**.

sock cymbals: Another name for hi-hat cymbals.

spring tension adjustment screw or **knob**: Used to adjust the tension/resistance of the foot pedal.

spurs: Attached to each side of the bass drum to help keep the drum from tilting side-to-side or sliding forward.

stick bag: Used for the storage and transportation of sticks, brushes and mallets.

tension adjustment knob: Used to adjust the tension or pressure of the snares.

tension rod: Used to hold the counterhoops in place and adjust the tension of the drumhead.

throw-off switch: Used to engage or disengage the snares from the head.

timbre: Tone color or quality.

tip (or **bead**): The front part of the drumstick used to strike the drum or cymbal.

toe technique: A technique for playing the hi-hat in which the heel is raised from the pedal while the ball of the foot is used to activate the hi-hat.

tom-tom mount: A device attached to the side of the tom-tom that secures it to the top of the bass drum.

tone control knob: Mounted on the outside of the shell of the snare drum (and some tom-toms) and attached to the internal muffler; when turned clockwise, the muffler presses against the batter head.

torque wrench: A type of drum key used to tune marching drums.

traditional grip: The right hand holds the stick with the palm down, while the left hand holds the stick with the palm up.

transparent: Clear

tuning: Changing or adjusting an instrument to sound at a specific pitch.